Withdrawn

EGYPTIAN GODS & GODDESSES

GODS AND GODDESSES OF MYTHOLOGY

EGYPTIAN GODS & GODDESSES

EDITED BY JOHNATHAN DEAVER

Britannica
Educational Publishing

IN ASSOCIATION WITH

ROSEN
EDUCATIONAL SERVICES

Published in 2014 by Britannica Educational Publishing (a trademark of Encyclopædia Britannica, Inc.) in association with The Rosen Publishing Group, Inc.
29 East 21st Street, New York, NY 10010

Distributed exclusively by Rosen Publishing.
To see additional Britannica Educational Publishing titles, go to http://www.rosenpublishing.com

First Edition

Britannica Educational Publishing
J. E. Luebering: Director, Core Reference Group
Anthony L. Green: Editor, Compton's by Britannica

Rosen Publishing
Hope Lourie Killcoyne: Executive Editor
Johnathan Deaver: Editor
Nelson Sá: Art Director
Brian Garvey: Designer
Cindy Reiman: Photography Manager

Cataloging-in-Publication Data

Egyptian gods & goddesses/edited by Johnathan Deaver.
     pages cm. — (Gods & goddesses of mythology)
Includes bibliographical references and index.
ISBN 978-1-62275-155-6 (library binding)
1. Gods, Egyptian. 2. Goddesses, Egyptian. 3. Mythology, Egyptian. 4. Egypt—Religion.
I. Deaver, Johnathan, editor of compilation. II. Title: Egyptian gods and goddesses.
BL2450.G6E39 2013
299'.31211—dc23
                                                                    2013026995

Manufactured in the United States of America

On the cover: Composite image of a statue of the deity Horus inside a corridor in an Egyptian temple. *YorkBerlin/Shutterstock.com (Horus statue), Paul Vinten/Shutterstock.com (temple interior)*

CONTENTS

Hieroglyphics and images of ritualistic animals and objects adorn an Egyptian manuscript found among the swathing of a mummy. Hulton Archive/Getty Images

INTRODUCTION

The ancient Egyptian religion was very complex. It was also relatively untouched by outside influences for many centuries. Its most striking feature was the vast number of gods and goddesses who could be depicted in human, animal, or other forms. The gods were never grouped systematically, and many of them were therefore interchangeable.

As they had different forms, the gods also personified different powers. Horus, a god in the form of a falcon, symbolized the sun and came to represent the pharaoh. Thoth, the moon god, was also the god of time because the phases of the moon were used to calculate the months. Powers of nature were symbolized by Re, the sun god; Nut, the sky goddess; and Geb, the Earth god. For a time Amenhotep IV made the sun, under the name Aton, the sole god.

A statue of the Egyptian god Horus outside the sandstone Temple of Horus at Edfu, Egypt. MyLoupe/Universal Images Group/Getty Images

Anubis, in the form of a dog, was god of the dead, Ptah was the creator, and Min was a god of fertility. Other major gods and goddesses included Bast, goddess of music; Isis, queen of the gods; Maat, the goddess of law, justice, and truth; Nekhbet, the protector of childbirth; Osiris, a

Papyrus from the Book of the Dead of Neferrenpet depicting a dead man with Anubis (second from left) *and other gods of the Underworld.* Werner Forman/Universal Images Group/Getty Images

fertility god, giver of civilization, and ruler of the dead; Sekhmet, a warlike sun goddess; and Shu, the god of light and air who supported the sky.

NATURE AND SIGNIFICANCE

Egyptian religious beliefs and practices were closely integrated into Egyptian society of the historical period (from *c.* 3000 BCE). Although there were probably many survivals from prehistory, these may be relatively unimportant for understanding later times because the transformation that established the Egyptian state created a new context for religion.

Religious phenomena were pervasive, so much so that it is not meaningful to view religion as a single entity that cohered as a system. Nevertheless, religion must be seen against a background of potentially nonreligious human activities and values. During its more than 3,000 years of development, Egyptian religion underwent significant changes of emphasis and practice, but in all periods religion had a clear consistency in character and style.

It is inappropriate to define religion narrowly, as consisting only in the cult of the gods and in human piety. Religious behaviour encompassed contact with the dead, practices such as divination and oracles, and magic, which mostly exploited divine instruments and associations.

There were two essential foci of public religion: the king and the gods. Both are among the most characteristic features of Egyptian civilization. The king had a unique status between humanity and the gods, partook in the world of the gods, and constructed great, religiously motivated funerary monuments for his afterlife. Egyptian gods are

11

renowned for their wide variety of forms, including animal forms and mixed forms with an animal head on a human body. The most important deities were the sun god, who had several names and aspects and was associated with many supernatural beings in a solar cycle modeled on the alternation of night and day, and Osiris, the god of the dead and ruler of the underworld. With his consort, Isis, Osiris became dominant in many contexts during the 1st millennium BCE, when solar worship was in relative decline.

The Egyptians conceived of the cosmos as including the gods and the present world—whose centre was, of course, Egypt—and as being surrounded by the realm of disorder, from which order had arisen and to which it would finally revert. Disorder had to be kept at bay. The task of the king as the protagonist of human society was to retain the benevolence of the gods in maintaining order against disorder. This ultimately pessimistic view of the cosmos was associated principally with the sun god and the solar cycle. It formed a powerful legitimation of king and elite in their task of preserving order.

Despite this pessimism, the official presentation of the cosmos on the monuments was positive and optimistic, showing the king and the gods in perpetual reciprocity and harmony. This implied contrast reaffirmed the fragile order. The restricted character of the monuments was also fundamental to a system of decorum that defined what could be shown, in what way it could be shown, and in what context. Decorum and the affirmation of order reinforced each other.

These beliefs are known from monuments and documents created by and for the king and the small elite. The beliefs and practices of the rest of the people are poorly known. While there is no reason to believe that there was a radical opposition between the beliefs of the elite and those of others, this possibility cannot be ruled out.

A painted wood statue of the goddess Isis. DEA Picture Library/Getty Images

Sources and Limitations of Ancient and Modern Knowledge

Ancient Egypt has been recovered archaeologically. Excavation and the recording of buildings have produced a great range of material, from large monuments to small objects and texts on perishable papyrus. Egyptian monuments are almost unique in the amount of inscription they bear; vast numbers of texts and representations with religious content are preserved, especially from the later 2nd and 1st millennia BCE. Much of this material is religious or has religious implications. This dominance may be misleading, partly because many monuments were in the desert, where they are well preserved, and partly because the lavishing of great resources on religious monuments for the king and the gods need not mean that people's lives were dominated by religion.

In addition to favouring large monuments and the elite, the archaeological record has other important biases. The formal cults of major deities and the realm of the dead are far better known than everyday religious activities, particularly those occurring in towns and villages, very few of which have been excavated. The absence of material deriving from the religious practice of most people in itself constitutes evidence suggesting both the inequality of society and the possibility, confirmed by other strands of evidence, that many people's religious life did not focus on official cult places and major temples.

Many official works of art present standard conceptions of the divine world and of the king's role in this world and in caring for the gods. Much religious evidence is at the same time artistic, and the production of works of art was a vital prestige concern of king and elite. Religious activities and rituals are less well known than this formalized artistic presentation of religious conceptions. The status of personal religion in the context of official cults is poorly understood.

Official forms were idealizing, and the untoward, which is everywhere an important focus of religion, was excluded almost entirely from them. The world of the monuments is that of Egypt alone, even though the Egyptians had normal, sometimes reciprocal, relations with other peoples. Decorum affected what was shown. Thus, the king was almost always depicted as the person offering to the gods, although temple rituals were performed by priests. Scenes of offering and of the gods conferring benefits on the king may not depict specific rituals, while the equal form in which king and gods are depicted bears no direct relation to real cult actions, which were performed on small cult images kept inside shrines.

An additional limitation is that knowledge of many central concerns was restricted. The king was stated to be alone in knowing aspects of the solar cycle. Knowledge of some religious texts was reserved to initiates, who would benefit from them both in this life and in the next. Magic evoked the power of the exotic and esoteric. Evidence for some restricted material is preserved, but it is not known who had access to it, while in other cases the restricted knowledge is only alluded to and is now inaccessible.

Death and the next world dominate both the archaeological record and popular modern conceptions of Egyptian religion. This dominance is determined to a great extent by the landscape of the country, since tombs were placed if possible in the desert. Vast resources were expended on creating prestigious burial places for absolute rulers or wealthy officials. Tombs contained elaborate grave goods (mostly plundered soon after deposition), representations of daily life or less commonly of religious subjects, and some texts that were intended to help the deceased attain the next world and prosper there. The texts came increasingly to be inscribed on coffins and stone sarcophagi or deposited in burials on papyrus. Some royal tombs included long passages from religious texts, many of them drawn from non-mortuary contexts and hence more broadly valuable as source material.

One crucial area where religion extended beyond narrow bounds was in the ethical instructions, which became the principal genre of Egyptian literature. These are known from the Middle Kingdom (c. 1900–1600 BCE) to the Roman period (1st century CE). As with other sources, the later texts are more overtly religious, but all show inextricable connections between proper conduct, the order of the world, and the gods.

KING, COSMOS, AND SOCIETY

The king was the centre of human society, the guarantor of order for the gods, the recipient of god-given benefits including life itself, and the benevolent ruler of the world for humanity. He was ultimately responsible for the cults of the dead, both for his predecessors in office and for the dead in general. His dominance in religion corresponded to his central political role: from late predynastic times (c. 3100 BCE), state organization was based on kingship and on the service of officials for the king. For humanity, the king had a superhuman role, being a manifestation of a god or of various deities on Earth.

The king's principal original title, the Horus name, proclaimed that he was an aspect of the chief god Horus, a sky god who was depicted as a falcon. Other identifications were added to this one, notably "Son of Re" (the sun god) and "Perfect God," both introduced in the 4th dynasty (c. 2575–2465 BCE), when the great pyramids were constructed.

The epithet "Son of Re" placed the king in a close but dependent relation with the leading figure in the pantheon. "Perfect God" (often rendered "Good God") indicated that the king had the status of a minor deity, for which he was "perfected" through accession to his office; it restricted the extent of his divinity and separated him from full deities.

In his intermediate position between humanity and the gods, the king could receive the most extravagant divine adulation and was in some ways more prominent than any single god. In death he aspired to full divinity but could not escape the human context. Although royal funerary monuments differed in type from other tombs and were vastly larger, they, too, were pillaged and vandalized, and few royal mortuary cults were long-lasting. Some kings, notably Amenhotep III (1390–53 BCE), Ramses II (1279–13 BCE), and several of the Ptolemies, sought deification during their own lifetime, while others, such as Amenemhet III (1818–c. 1770 BCE), became minor gods after their death, but these developments show how restricted royal divinity was. The divinized king coexisted with his mortal self, and as many nonroyal individuals as kings became deified after death.

The gods, the king, humanity, and the dead existed together in the cosmos, which the creator god had brought into being from the preexistent chaos. All living beings, except perhaps the creator, would die at the end of time. The sun god became aged and needed to be rejuvenated and reborn daily. The ordered cosmos was surrounded by and shot through with disorder, which had to be kept at bay. Disorder menaced most strongly at such times of transition as the passage from one year to the next or the death of a king. Thus, the king's role in maintaining order was cosmic and not merely social. His exaction of service from people was necessary to the cosmos.

CHAPTER 1

AN INTRODUCTION TO THE DEITIES

Egyptian religion was polytheistic. The gods who inhabited the bounded and ultimately perishable cosmos varied in nature and capacity. The word *netjer* ("god") described a much wider range of beings than the deities of monotheistic religions, including what might be termed demons. As is almost necessary in polytheism, gods were neither all-powerful nor all-knowing. Their power was immeasurably greater than that of human beings, and they had the ability to live almost indefinitely, survive fatal wounds, be in more than one place at once, affect people in visible and invisible ways, and so forth.

Most gods were generally benevolent, but their favour could not be counted on, and they had to be propitiated and encouraged to inhabit their cult images so that they could receive the cult and further the reciprocity of divine and human. Some deities, notably such goddesses as Neith, Sekhmet, and Mut, had strongly ambivalent characters. The god Seth embodied the disordered aspects of the ordered world, and in the 1st millennium BCE he came to be seen as an enemy who had to be eliminated (but would remain present).

The characters of the gods were not neatly defined. Most had a principal association, such as that of Re with the sun or that of the goddess Hathor with women, but there was much overlap, especially among the leading deities. In general, the more closely circumscribed a deity's character, the less powerful that deity was. All the main gods acquired the characteristics of creator gods. A single figure could have many names; among those of the sun god, the most important were Khepri (the morning form),

Depiction of Hathor, located in the Mortuary Temple of Hatshepsut, Deir el-Bahari, Egypt. iStockphoto/Thinkstock

Re-Harakhty (a form of Re associated with Horus), and Atum (the old, evening form). There were three principal "social" categories of deity: gods, goddesses, and youthful deities, mostly male.

Gods had regional associations, corresponding to their chief cult places. The sun god's cult place was Heliopolis, Ptah's was Memphis, and Amon's was Thebes. These were not necessarily their original cult places. The principal cult of Khnum, the creator god who formed people from clay like a potter, was Elephantine, and he was the lord of the nearby First Cataract. His cult is not attested there before the New Kingdom, however, even though he was important from the 1st dynasty (*c.* 2925–2775 BCE). The main earlier sanctuary there belonged to the goddess Satet, who became Khnum's companion. Similarly, Mut, the partner of Amon at Thebes, seems to have originated elsewhere.

The chief form in which gods were represented was human, and many deities had only human form. Among these deities were very ancient figures such as the fertility god Min and the creator and craftsman Ptah. The cosmic gods Shu, of the air and sky, and Geb, of Earth, had human form, as did Osiris, Isis, and Nephthys, deities who provided a model of human society. In temple reliefs the gods were depicted in human form, which was central to decorum. Gods having animal manifestations were therefore shown with a human body and the head of their animal. The opposite convention, a human head and an animal body, was used for the king, who was shown as a sphinx with a lion's body. Sphinxes could receive other heads, notably those of rams and falcons, associating the form with Amon and Re-Harakhty. Demons were represented in more

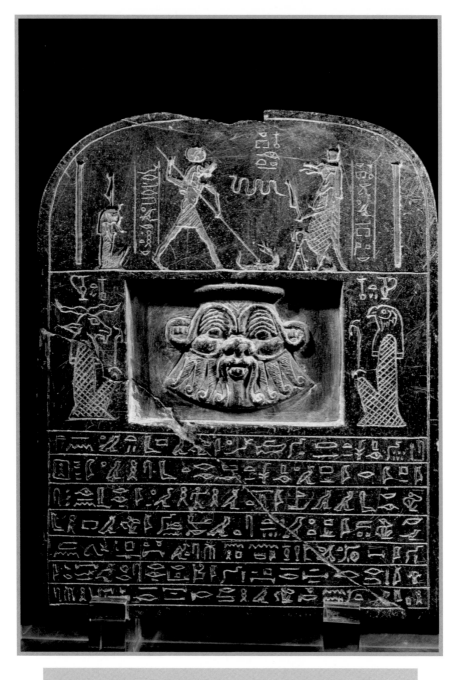

Relief detailing the god Bes (center) *and Khnum* (left). Werner Forman/Universal Images Group/Getty Images

extravagant forms and combinations; these became common in the 1st millennium BCE. Together with the cult of animals, they were mocked by Greek and Roman writers.

Apart from major deities—gods who received a cult or had a significant cosmic role—there were important minor figures. Several of these marginal beings had grotesque forms and variable names. The most prominent were Bes, a helpful figure with dwarf form and a mask-like face, associated especially with women and children, and Taurt, a goddess with similar associations whose physical form combined features of a hippopotamus and a crocodile. Among demons, the most important figure was Apopis, shown as a colossal snake, who was the enemy of the sun god in his daily cycle through the cosmos. Apopis existed outside the ordered realm; he had to be defeated daily, but, since he did not belong to the sphere of existence, he could not be destroyed.

GROUPINGS OF DEITIES

The number of deities was large and was not fixed. New ones appeared, and some ceased to be worshipped. Deities were grouped in various ways. The most ancient known grouping is the Ennead, which is probably attested from the 3rd dynasty (c. 2650–2575 BCE). Enneads were groups of nine deities, nine being the "plural" of three (in Egypt the number three symbolized plurality in general); not all Enneads consisted of nine gods.

The principal Ennead was the Great Ennead of Heliopolis. This was headed by the sun god and creator Re or Re-Atum, followed by Shu and Tefnut, deities of air and moisture; Geb and Nut, who represented Earth and sky; and Osiris, Isis, Seth, and Nephthys. This ordering incorporated a myth of creation, to which was joined the myth of Osiris, whose deeds and attributes ranged from the founding of civilization to kinship, kingship, and succession to office. The Ennead excluded the successor figure, Horus, son of Osiris, who is essential to the meaning of the myth. Thus, the Ennead has the appearance of a grouping that brought together existing religious conceptions but was rather arbitrary and inflexible, perhaps because of the significance of the number nine.

Relief detailing the pharaoh making offerings before goddess Tefnut (left) *and god Ptah* (middle), *located at the Medinet Habu temple in Egypt.* Universal Images Group/Getty Images

Other numerical ordering schemas included the Ogdoad (group of eight gods) of Hermopolis, which embodied the inchoate world before creation and consisted of four pairs of male and female deities with abstract names such as Darkness, Absence, and Endlessness. Here, too, the number was significant in itself because at least six different pairs of names are known although eight deities are listed in any occurrence. The major god Amon, whose name can mean "He who is hidden," was often one of the Ogdoad with his female counterpart, Amaunet.

The most common grouping, principally in the New Kingdom and later, was the triad. The archetypal triad of Osiris, Isis, and Horus exhibits the normal pattern of a god and a goddess with a youthful deity, usually male. Most local centres came to have triads, the second and third members of which might be devised for the sake of form. Thus, one triad worshipped in the Greco-Roman-period temple at Kawm Umbu (Kôm Ombo) consisted of Haroeris (the "elder Horus"), the goddess Tsenetnofret ("the perfect companion"), and the youthful god Pnebtawy ("the lord of the two lands"). The last name, which is an epithet of kings, is revealing because youthful gods had many attributes of kings. As this case indicates, triads resemble a minimal nuclear family, but deities were rarely spouses. The notion of plurality and the bringing together of the essential types of deity may have been as important to the triads as the family analogy.

Another important ordering of deities was syncretism, a term with a special meaning for Egyptian religion. Two or more names of gods were often combined to form a composite identity; many combinations included the name of Re. Prominent examples are Amon-Re, a

Painted relief detailing Amon-Re (left) *and Rameses III, located in the Medinet Habu temple, Egypt.* Universal Images Group/Getty Images

fusion of Amon and Re, and Osiris-Apis, a fusion of Osiris with the Apis bull. Although composite forms such as Amon-Re became the principal identities of some gods, the separate deities continued to exist and sometimes, as in the case of Re, to receive a cult. In part, these syncretisms expressed the idea of Amon in his aspect as Re; they were thus analogous to the multiple manifestations of individual deities. Through syncretism many major deities came to resemble one another more closely.

CHAPTER 2 WORSHIP

Most cults centred on the daily tending and worship of an image of a deity and were analogous to the pattern of human life. The shrine containing the image was opened at dawn, and then the deity was purified, greeted and praised, clothed, and fed. There were several further services, and the image was finally returned to its shrine for the night. Apart from this activity, which took place within the temple and was performed by a small group of priests, there were numerous festivals at which the shrine and image were taken out from the sanctuary on a portable barque, becoming visible to the people and often visiting other temples. Thus, the daily cult was a state concern, whose function was to maintain reciprocity between the human and the divine, largely in isolation from the people. This reciprocity was fundamental because deities and humanity together sustained the cosmos. If the gods were not satisfied, they might cease to inhabit their images and retreat to their other abode, the sky. Temples were constructed as microcosms whose purity and wholeness symbolized the proper order of the larger world outside.

The priesthood became increasingly important. In early periods there seem to have been no full-time professional priests; people could hold part-time high priestly offices, or they could have humbler positions on a rotating basis, performing duties for one month in four. The chief officiant may have been a professional.

While performing their duties, priests submitted to rules of purity and abstinence. One result of this system was that more people were involved in the cult and had access to the temple than would have been the case if there had been a permanent staff. Although most priestly positions were for men, women were involved in the cult of the goddess Hathor, and in the New Kingdom and later many women held the title of "chantress" of a deity (perhaps often a courtesy title); they were principally involved in musical cult performances.

Festivals allowed more direct interaction between people and the gods. Questions were often asked of a deity, and a response might be given by a forward or backward movement of the barque carried on the priests' shoulders. Oracles, of which this was one form, were invoked by the king to obtain sanction for his plans, including military campaigns abroad and important appointments. Although evidence is sparse, consultation with deities may have been part of religious interaction in all periods and for all levels of society.

Apart from this interaction between deities and individual people or groups, festivals were times of communal celebration and often of the public reenactment of myths, such as the death and vindication of Osiris at Abydos or the defeat of Seth by Horus at Idfu. They had both a personal and a general social role in the spectrum of religious practice.

Nonetheless, the main audience for the most important festivals of the principal gods of state held in capital cities may have been the ruling elite rather than the people as a whole. In the New Kingdom these cities were remodeled as vast cosmic stages for the enactment of royal-divine relations and rituals.

Piety, Practical Religion, and Magic

Despite the importance of temples and their architectural dominance, the evidence for cult does not point to mass participation in temple religion. The archaeological material may be misleading because in addition to major temples there were many local sanctuaries that may have responded more directly to the concerns and needs of those who lived around them. From some periods numerous votive offerings are preserved from a few temples. Among these are Early Dynastic and Old Kingdom provincial temples, but the fullest evidence is from New Kingdom temples of Hathor at Thebes and several frontier sites and from the Late and Ptolemaic periods (664–30 BCE).

Although votive offerings show that significant numbers of people took gifts to temples, it is difficult to gauge the social status of donors, whose intentions are seldom indicated, probably in part for reasons of decorum. Two likely motives are disinterested pious donation for the deity and offering in the hope of obtaining a specific benefit. Many New Kingdom offerings to Hathor relate to human fertility and thus belong to the second of these categories. Late period bronze statuettes are often inscribed with a formula requesting that the deity represented should "give life" to the donor, without stating a specific need. These may be more generally pious donations, among which can also be counted nonroyal dedications of small parcels of land to temples. These donations are recorded on stelae from the New Kingdom onward. They parallel the massive royal endowments to temples of land and other resources, which resulted in their becoming very powerful economic and political institutions.

Apart from the donation of offerings to conventional cult temples, there was a vast Late period expansion in animal cults. These might be more or less closely related to major deities. They involved a variety of practices centring on the mummification and burial of animals. The principal bull cults, which gave important oracles, focused on a single animal kept in a special shrine. The burial of an Apis bull was a major occasion involving vast expenditure. Some animals, such as the sacred ibis (connected with

A painted limestone stele of the god Apis in piety before the Apis bull. DEA/G. Dagli Orti/De Agostini/Getty Images

Thoth), were kept, and buried, in millions. The dedication of a burial seems to have counted as a pious act. The best-known area for these cults and associated practices is the necropolis of northern Saqqarah, which served the city of Memphis. Numerous species were buried there, and people visited the area to consult oracles and spend the night in a temple area and receive healing dreams. A few people resided permanently in the animal necropolis in a state akin to monastic seclusion.

There are two further important groups of evidence for pious and reciprocal relations between people and gods. One is proper names of all periods, the majority of which are meaningful utterances with religious content. For example, names state that deities "show favour" to or "love" a child or its parents. From the end of the New Kingdom (c. 1100 BCE), names commonly refer to consultation of oracles during pregnancy, alluding to a different mode of human-divine relations. The second source is a group of late New Kingdom inscriptions recounting episodes of affliction that led to people's perceiving that they had wronged a god. These texts, which provide evidence of direct pious relations, are often thought to show a transformation of religious attitudes in that period, but allusions to similar relations in Middle Kingdom texts suggest that the change was as much in what was written down as in basic attitudes.

Piety was one of many modes of religious action and relations. Much of religion concerned attempts to comprehend and respond to the unpredictable and unfortunate. The activities involved often took place away from temples and are little known. In later periods, there was an increasing concentration of religious practice around temples; for earlier times evidence is sparse. The essential questions people asked, as in many religious traditions, were why

Bronze statuette representing the god Thoth as an ibis. DEA/G. Dagli Orti/De Agostini/Getty Images

something had happened and why it had happened to them, what would be an appropriate response, what agency they should turn to, and what might happen in the future. To obtain answers to these questions, people turned to oracles and other forms of divination, such as consulting seers or calendars of lucky and unlucky days. From the New Kingdom and later, questions to oracles are preserved, often on such mundane matters as whether someone should cultivate a particular field in a given year. These cannot have been presented only at festivals, and priests must have addressed oracular questions to gods within their sanctuaries. Oracles of gods also played an important part in dispute settlement and litigation in some communities.

A vital focus of questioning was the world of the dead. The recently deceased might exert influence on the living for good or for bad. Offerings to the dead, which were required by custom, were intended, among other purposes, to make them well disposed. People occasionally deposited with their offerings a letter telling the deceased of their problems and asking for assistance. A few of these letters are complaints to the deceased person, alleging that he or she is afflicting the writer. This written communication with the dead was confined to the very few literate members of the population, but it was probably part of a more widespread oral practice. Some tombs of prominent people acquired minor cults that may have originated in frequent successful recourse to them for assistance.

Offerings to the dead generally did not continue long after burial, and most tombs were robbed within a generation or so. Thus, relations with dead kin probably focused on the recently deceased. Nonetheless, the dead were respected and feared more widely. The attitudes attested are almost uniformly negative. The dead were held accountable for much misfortune, both on a local and domestic level and in the broader context of the state. People were also concerned that when they died, those in the next world would oppose their entry to it as newcomers who might oust the less recently dead. These attitudes show that, among many possible modes of existence after death, an important conception was one in which the dead remained near the living and could return and disturb them. Such beliefs are rare in the official mortuary literature.

A prominent aspect of practical religion was magic. There is no meaningful distinction between Egyptian religion and magic. Magic was a force present in the world from the beginning of creation and was personified as the god Heka, who received a cult in some regions. Magic could be invoked by using appropriate means and was generally positive, being valuable for counteracting misfortune and in seeking to achieve ends for which unseen help was necessary. Magic also formed part of the official cult. It could, however, be used for antisocial purposes as well as benign ones. There is a vast range of evidence for magical practice, from amulets to elaborate texts. Much magic from the Greco-Roman period mixed Egyptian and foreign materials and invoked new and exotic beings. Preserved magical texts record elite magic rather than general practice. Prominent among magical practitioners, both in folklore and, probably, in real life, were "lector priests," the officiants in temple cults who had privileged access to written texts. Most of the vast corpus of funerary texts was magical in character.

THE WORLD OF THE DEAD

The majority of evidence from ancient Egypt comes from funerary monuments and burials of royalty, of the elite, and, for the Late period, of animals; relatively little is known of the mortuary practices of the mass of the population. Reasons for this dominance of the tomb include both the desert location of burials and the use of mortuary structures for display among the living. Alongside the fear of the dead, there was a moral community between the living and the dead, so the dead were an essential part of society, especially in the 3rd and 2nd millennia BCE.

The basic purpose of mortuary preparation was to ensure a safe and successful passage into the hereafter. Belief in an afterlife and a passage to it is evident in predynastic burials, which are oriented to the west (the domain of the dead), and which include pottery grave goods as well as personal possessions of the deceased. The most striking development of later mortuary practice was mummification, which was related to a belief that the body must continue intact for the deceased to live in the next world. Mummification evolved gradually from the Old Kingdom to the early 1st millennium BCE, after which it declined. It was too elaborate and costly ever to be available to the majority.

This decline of mortuary practice was part of the more general shift in the focus of religious life toward the temples and toward more communal forms. It has been suggested tentatively that belief in the afterlife became less strong in the 1st millennium BCE. Whether or not this is true, it is clear that in various periods some people voiced skepticism about the existence of a blessed afterlife and the necessity for mortuary provision, but the provision nevertheless continued to the end.

It was thought that the next world might be located in the area around the tomb (and consequently near the living); on the "perfect ways of the West," as it is expressed in Old Kingdom invocations; among the stars or in the celestial regions with the sun god; or in the underworld, the domain of Osiris. One prominent notion was that of the "Elysian Fields," where the deceased could enjoy an ideal agricultural existence in a marshy land of plenty. The journey to the next world was fraught with obstacles. It could be imagined as a passage by ferry past a succession of portals, or through an "Island of Fire." One crucial test was the judgment after death, a subject often depicted from the New Kingdom onward. The date of origin of this belief is uncertain, but it was probably no later than the late Old Kingdom. The related text, Chapter 125 of the Book of the Dead, responded magically to the dangers of the judgment, which assessed the deceased's conformity with *maat* "order." Those who failed the judgment would "die a second time" and would be cast outside the ordered cosmos. In the demotic story of Setna (3rd century BCE), this notion of moral retribution acquired overtones similar to those of the Christian judgment after death.

AKHENATON

Akhenaton was a king (1353–36 BCE) of ancient Egypt of the 18th dynasty who established a new cult dedicated to the Aton, the sun's disc (hence his assumed name, Akhenaton, meaning "beneficial to Aton").

Relief depicting Akhenaten as a sphinx making an offering to the sun god Aton. Werner Forman/Universal Images Group/Getty Images

AMON

Amon may have been originally one of the eight deities of the Hermopolite creation myth; his cult reached Thebes, where he became the patron of the pharaohs by the reign of Mentuhotep I (2008–1957 BCE). At that date he was already identified with the sun god Re of Heliopolis and, as Amon-Re, was received as a national god. Represented in human form, sometimes with a ram's head, or as a ram, Amon-Re was worshipped as part of the Theban triad, which included a goddess, Mut, and a youthful god, Khons. His temple at Karnak was among the largest and wealthiest in the land from the New Kingdom (1539–c. 1075 BCE) onward. Local forms of Amon were also worshipped at the Temple of

Relief of Amon at the temple of Ramses III. DEA/S. Amantini/De Agostini/ Getty Images

UNDERSTANDING THE HIEROGLYPH

The hieroglyph was a character used in a system of pictorial writing, particularly that form used on ancient Egyptian monuments. Hieroglyphic symbols may represent the objects that they depict but usually stand for particular sounds or groups of sounds. *Hieroglyph*, meaning "sacred carving," is a Greek translation of the Egyptian phrase "the god's words," which was used at the time of the early Greek contacts with Egypt to distinguish the older hieroglyphs from the handwriting of the day (demotic). Modern usage has extended the term to other writing systems, such as Hieroglyphic Hittite, Mayan hieroglyphs, and early Cretan. There is no connection between Egyptian hieroglyphs and these other scripts, the only certain derivative from the Egyptian writing being that used for Meroitic.

Egyptian hieroglyphic writing was composed entirely of pictures, though the object depicted cannot be identified in every instance. The earliest examples that can be read show the hieroglyphs used as actual writing, that is, with phonetic values, and not as picture writing such as that of the Eskimos or American Indians. The origins of the script are not known. It apparently arose in the late pre-dynastic period (just before 2925 BCE). There were contacts between Egypt and Mesopotamia at this time, and it has been thought that the concept of writing was borrowed from the Sumerians. This is certainly possible, but, even if this was the case, the two systems were so different in their use of signs that it is clear that they developed independently.

Except for names and a few titles, the oldest inscriptions cannot be read. In many cases individual hieroglyphs were used that are familiar from later periods, but the meaning of the inscription as a whole is obscure. It is apparent that this writing did not represent the sounds as completely as was the case later.

In the period of the 3rd dynasty (*c.* 2650–*c.* 2575 BCE), many of the principles of hieroglyphic writing were regularized. From that time on, until the script was supplanted by an early version of Coptic (about the 3rd and 4th centuries CE), the system remained virtually unchanged. Even the number of signs used remained constant at about 700 for more than 2,000 years. With the rise of Christianity in the 2nd and 3rd centuries CE came the decline and ultimate demise not only of the ancient Egyptian religion but of its hieroglyphics as well. The use, by the Egyptian Christians, of an adapted form of the Greek alphabet, caused a correspondingly widespread disuse of the native Egyptian script. The last known use of hieroglyphics is on an inscription dated 394 CE.

Hieroglyphic writing followed four basic principles. First, a hieroglyph could be used in an almost purely pictorial way. The sign of a man with his hand to his mouth might stand for the word "eat." Similarly, the word "sun" would be represented by a large circle with a smaller circle in its centre. Second, a hieroglyph might represent or imply another word suggested by the picture. The sign for "sun" could as easily serve as the sign for "day" or as the name of the sun god Re. The sign for "eat" could also represent the more conceptual word "silent" by suggesting the covering of the mouth. Third, the signs also served as representatives of words that shared consonants in the same order. Thus the Egyptian words for "man" and "be bright," both spelled with the same consonants could be rendered by the same hieroglyph. Fourth, the hieroglyphs stood for individual or combinations of consonants.

It is arguable whether the ancient Greeks or Romans understood hieroglyphics. The Greeks almost certainly did not, since, from their viewpoint, hieroglyphics were not phonetic signs but symbols of a more abstruse and allegorical nature. The humanist revival of the European Middle Ages, although it produced a set of Italian-designed hieroglyphics, gave no further insight into the original Egyptian ones.

The first attempt to decipher hieroglyphics, based on the assumption that they were indeed phonetic symbols, was made by the German scholar Athanasius Kircher in the mid-1600s. Despite his initial correct hypothesis, he correctly identified only one symbol.

The discovery of the Rosetta Stone in 1799 was to provide the key to the final unlocking of the mystery. The stone was inscribed with three different scripts: hieroglyphic, demotic, and Greek. Based on the stone's own declaration, in the Greek portion, that the text was identical in all three cases, several significant advances were made in translation. A.I. Silvestre de Sacy, a French scholar, and J.D. Akerblad, a Swedish diplomat, succeeded in identifying a number of proper names in the demotic text. Akerblad also correctly assigned phonetic values to a few of the signs. An Englishman, Thomas Young, correctly identified five of the hieroglyphics. The full deciphering of the stone was accomplished by another Frenchman, Jean-Françoise Champollion. He brought to the stone a natural facility for languages (having, by age 16, become proficient in six ancient Oriental languages as well as Greek and Latin). By comparison of one sign with another, he was able to determine the phonetic values of the hieroglyphics. Later studies simply confirmed and refined Champollion's work.

Luxor on the east bank of Thebes and at Madinat Habu (Medinet Habu) on the west bank.

Amon's name meant the Hidden One, and his image was painted blue to denote invisibility. This attribute of invisibility led to a popular belief during the New Kingdom in the knowledge and impartiality of Amon, making him a god for those who felt oppressed.

Amon's influence was, in addition, closely linked to the political well-being of Egypt. During the Hyksos domination (*c.* 1630–*c.* 1523 BCE), the princes of Thebes sustained his worship. Following the Theban victory over the Hyksos and the creation of an empire, Amon's stature and the wealth of his temples grew. In the late 18th dynasty Akhenaton (Amenhotep IV) directed his religious reform against the traditional cult of Amon, but he was unable to convert people from their belief in Amon and the other gods, and, under Tutankhamen, Ay, and Horemheb (1332–1292 BCE), Amon was gradually restored as the god of the empire and patron of the pharaoh.

In the New Kingdom, religious speculation among Amon's priests led to the concept of Amon as part of a triad (with Ptah and Re) or as a single god of whom all the other gods, even Ptah and Re, were manifestations. Under the sacerdotal state ruled by the priests of Amon at Thebes (c. 1075–c. 950 BCE), Amon evolved into a universal god who intervened through oracles in many affairs of state.

The succeeding 22nd and 23rd dynasties, the invasion of Egypt by Assyria (671–c. 663 BCE), and the sack of Thebes (c. 663 BCE) did not reduce the stature of the cult, which had acquired a second main centre at Tanis in the Nile River delta. Moreover, the worship of Amon had become established among the inhabitants of Kush in the Sudan, who were accepted by Egyptian worshippers of Amon when they invaded Egypt and ruled as the 25th dynasty (715–664 BCE). From this period onward, resistance to foreign occupation of Egypt was strongest in Thebes. Amon's cult spread to the oases, especially Siwa in Egypt's western desert, where Amon was linked with Jupiter. Alexander the Great won acceptance as pharaoh by consulting the oracle at Siwa, and he also rebuilt the sanctuary of Amon's temple at Luxor. The early Ptolemaic rulers contained Egyptian nationalism by supporting the temples, but, starting with Ptolemy IV Philopator in 207 BCE, nationalistic rebellions in Upper Egypt erupted. During the revolt of 88–85 BCE, Ptolemy IX Soter II sacked Thebes, dealing Amon's cult a severe blow. In 27 BCE a strong earthquake devastated the Theban temples, while in the Greco-Roman world the cult of Isis and Osiris gradually displaced that of Amon.

ANUBIS

Also called Anpu, Anubis was the ancient Egyptian god of the dead, represented by a jackal or the figure of a man with the head of a jackal. In the Early Dynastic period and the Old Kingdom, he enjoyed a preeminent (though not exclusive) position as lord of the dead, but he was later overshadowed by Osiris. His role is reflected in such epithets as "He Who Is upon His Mountain" (i.e., the necropolis), "Lord of the Sacred Land," "Foremost of the Westerners," and "He Who Is in the Place of Embalming."

His particular concern was with the funerary cult and the care of the dead; hence, he was reputed to be the inventor of embalming, an art he first employed on the corpse of Osiris. In his later role as the "conductor of souls," he was sometimes identified by the Greco-Roman world with the Greek Hermes in the composite deity Hermanubis.

Wooden statue of Anubis upon a gilded chest. DEA/S. Vannini/De Agostini/Getty Images

APOPIS

A popis, also spelled Apophis or Apopi, was the Hyksos king of ancient Egypt (reigned c. 1585–42 BCE), who initially controlled much of Egypt but was driven back northward to the vicinity of his capital in the Nile River delta by the successive attacks of the Theban pharaohs.

Apopis is attested in Upper Egypt by stone fragments from Al-Gabalayn. A literary tale concerning Apopis and the Theban king Seqenenre portrays the Thebans as vassals of the Hyksos ruler, but this probably does not reflect historical reality. Egyptians and Hyksos peacefully coexisted for some time, as the Thebans seem to have grazed their cattle in the Nile delta, which was ruled by the Hyksos.

War may have erupted between Apopis and Seqenenre, as the Theban king's mummy displays terrible head wounds. His successor, Kamose, declared a Middle Egyptian town as his northern frontier. He carried on the war, as is shown by two monuments from Thebes, and

THE MEANING OF THE SCARAB

In ancient Egyptian religion, the scarab was an important symbol in the form of the dung beetle (*Scarabaeus sacer*), which lays its eggs in dung balls fashioned through rolling. This beetle was associated with the divine manifestation of the early morning sun, Khepri, whose name was written with the scarab hieroglyph and who was believed to roll the disc of the morning sun over the eastern horizon at day-break. Since the scarab hieroglyph, Kheper, refers variously to the ideas of existence, manifestation, development, growth, and effectiveness, the beetle itself was a favourite form used for amulets in all periods of Egyptian history.

Scarabs of various materials, glazed steatite being most common, form an important class of Egyptian antiquities. Such objects usually have the bases inscribed or decorated with designs and are simultaneously amulets and seals. Though they first appeared in the late Old Kingdom (c. 2575–c. 2130 BCE), when they evolved from the so-called button seals, scarabs remained rare until Middle Kingdom times (1938–c. 1630 BCE), when they were fashioned in great numbers. Some were used simply as ornaments, while others were purely amuletic in purpose, as the large basalt "heart scarabs" of the New Kingdom (1539–1075 BCE) and later times, which were placed in the bandages of mummies and were symbolically identified with the heart of the deceased. A winged scarab might also be placed on the breast of the mummy, and later a number of other scarabs were placed about the body.

The seal type of scarab was, however, the most common, and many clay sealings have been found attesting to this use. Spiral motifs and titles of officials are characteristic of Middle Kingdom examples, while on later scarabs a wide variety of designs and inscriptions are found. The inscriptions are sometimes mottoes referring to places, deities, and so on or containing words of good omen or friendly wishes. Historically, the most valuable class of scarabs is that which bears royal names; these ranged in date from the 11th dynasty to the Late period. The names of the Hyksos dynasts have been largely recovered from collections of scarabs.

A related type of seal amulet, called by Egyptologists the scaraboid, was similar in shape but lacked the details of the beetle's anatomy. Egyptian scarabs were carried by trade throughout the eastern Mediterranean and to Mesopotamia. Numerous examples of Greek and Etruscan imitations have also been found.

drove the Hyksos northward to the vicinity of Memphis (near Cairo). A Theban fleet also sailed by Avaris, Apopis's delta capital.

Apopis reacted by calling on his ally to the south, the Kushite prince, to attack the Thebans in their rear. His messenger, however, was intercepted, and his plan was thwarted by Kamose. Some time soon after this raid, but before the final Hyksos expulsion, Apopis died.

ATON

A ton, also spelled Aten, was a sun god, depicted as the solar disc emitting rays terminating in human hands, whose worship briefly was the state religion. The pharaoh Akhenaton (reigned 1353–36 BCE) returned to supremacy of the sun god, with the startling innovation that the Aton was to be the only god. To remove himself from the pre-eminent cult of Amon-Re at Thebes, Akhenaton built the city Akhetaton (now Tell el-Amarna) as the centre for the Aton's worship.

The most important surviving document of the new religion is the Aton Hymn, which was inscribed in several versions in the tombs of Akhetaton. Like some other hymns of its period, the text focuses on the world of nature and the god's beneficent provision for it. The hymn opens with the rising of the sun:

> *"Men had slept like the dead; now they lift their arms in praise, birds fly, fish leap, plants bloom, and work begins. Aton creates the son in the mother's womb, the seed in men, and has generated all life. He has distinguished the races, their natures, tongues, and skins, and fulfills the needs of all. Aton made the Nile in Egypt and rain, like a heavenly Nile, in foreign countries. He has a million forms according to the time of day and from where he is seen; yet he is always the same."*

The only people who know and comprehend the god fully are said to be Akhenaton together with his wife, Nefertiti. The hymn to the Aton has been compared in imagery to Psalm 104 ("Bless the Lord, O my soul").

Akhenaton devoted himself to the worship of the Aton, erasing all images of Amon and all writings of his name and sometimes even writings containing the word "gods." But the new religion was rejected by the Egyptian elite after Akhenaton's death, and the general populace had probably never adopted it in the first place. After Akhenaton's death, the old gods were reestablished and the new city abandoned. Aton worship was not fully monotheistic (because the pharaoh himself was considered a god), nor was it a direct precursor of monotheistic religions such as Judaism.

ATUM

Atum was one of the manifestations of the sun and creator god, perhaps originally a local deity of Heliopolis. Atum's myth merged with that of the great sun god Re, giving rise to the deity Re-Atum. When distinguished from Re, Atum was the creator's original form, living inside Nun, the primordial waters of chaos. At creation he emerged to engender himself and the gods. He was identified with the setting sun and was shown as an aged figure who had to be regenerated during the night, to appear as Khepri at dawn and as Re at the sun's zenith.

Wooden slab illustrating lady Taperet praying to Atum. DEA/G. Dagli Orti/De Agostini/ Getty Images

HAPI

Hapi was the personification of the annual inundation of the Nile River. Hapi was the most important among numerous personifications of aspects of natural fertility, and his dominance increased during Egyptian history. Hymns were composed in his honour, but he had no temples or formal cult except at the narrows of Jabal al-Silsila in the south, where shrines were built and offerings were cast annually into the river's rising waters. Hapi was represented as a fat man with swelling, pendulous breasts (as an indication of prosperity), dressed in a belt suitable to a marsh dweller or servant. This form, which was originally common to many personifications, became identified increasingly closely with Hapi.

BASTET

Bastet, also called Bast, was worshipped in the form of a lioness and later a cat. The daughter of Re, the sun god, Bastet was an ancient deity whose ferocious nature was ameliorated after the domestication of the cat around 1500 BCE. She was native to Bubastis in the Nile River delta but also had an important cult at Memphis. In the Late and Ptolemaic periods large cemeteries of mummified cats were created at both sites, and thousands of bronze statuettes of the goddess were deposited as votive offerings. Small figures of cats were also worn as amulets; this, too, was probably related to the cult of Bastet.

Bronze figure of Bastet holding a lion-headed aegis. Werner Forman/Universal Images Group/Getty Images

51

BES

Bes, a minor god of ancient Egypt, was represented as a dwarf with large head, goggle eyes, protruding tongue, bowlegs, bushy tail, and usually a crown of feathers. The name "Bes" is now used to designate a group of deities of similar appearance with a wide variety of ancient names. The god's figure was that of a grotesque mountebank and was intended to inspire joy or drive away pain and sorrow, his hideousness being perhaps supposed to scare away evil spirits. He was portrayed on mirrors, ointment vases, and other personal articles. He was associated with music and with childbirth and was represented in the "birth houses" devoted to the cult of the child god. Contrary to the usual rule of representation, Bes was commonly shown full-faced rather than in profile, since full-faced figures were marginal to the normal, ordered world.

GEB

G eb was the god of Earth, the physical support of the
world. Geb constituted, along with Nut, his sister,
the second generation in the Ennead (group of nine gods)
of Heliopolis. In Egyptian art Geb, as a portrayal of Earth,
was often depicted lying by the feet of Shu, the air god,

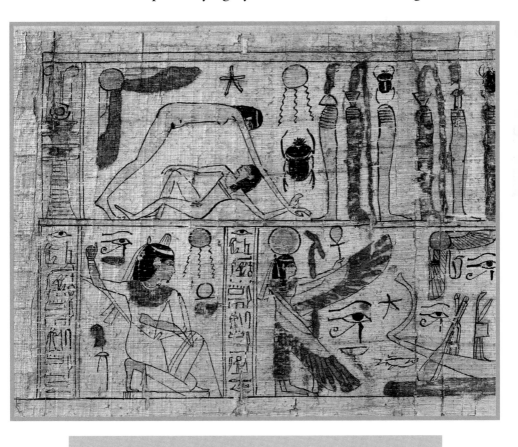

*Funerary papyrus detailing the creation of the world with Geb arched
above Nut.* DEA/G. Dagli Orti/De Agostini/Getty Images

HEKA

In ancient Egyptian religion, Heka was the personification of one of the attributes of the creator god Re-Atum; the term is usually translated as "magic," or "magical power," though its exact meaning pertains to cult practice as well. Heka was believed to accompany Re in his solar boat on its daily trip across the heavens; it could also be given to and used by common men. The Egyptians believed that heka was the primordial force present at the creation of the world, that it could be summoned up during the observance of religious ritual, and that its chief function was the preservation of the natural world order.

with Nut, the goddess of the sky, arched above them. Geb was usually portrayed as a man without any distinguishing characteristics, but at times he was represented with his head surmounted by a goose, the hieroglyph of his name. He was the third divine ruler among the gods; the human pharaohs claimed to be descended from him, and the royal throne was referred to as "the throne of Geb."

HATHOR

Hathor was the goddess of the sky, of women, and of fertility and love. Hathor's worship originated in Early Dynastic times (3rd millennium BCE). The name "Hathor" means "estate of Horus" and may not be her original name. Her principal animal form was that of a cow, and she was strongly associated with motherhood. Hathor was closely connected with the sun god Re of Heliopolis, whose "eye" or daughter she was said to be. In her cult centre at Dandarah in Upper Egypt, she was worshipped with Horus.

There were cults of Hathor in many towns in Egypt and also abroad, for she was the patroness of foreign parts and of many minerals won from the desert. In the Sinai turquoise mines, for example, she was called "Lady of Turquoise." At Dayr al-Bahri, in the necropolis of Thebes, she became "Lady of the West" and patroness of the region of the dead. In the Late period (1st millennium BCE), women aspired to be assimilated with Hathor in the next world, as men aspired to become Osiris. The Greeks identified Hathor with their Aphrodite.

Column capital carved with the head of Hathor in her cow form, located in the kiosk of Pharaoh Nectanebo I in Egypt. Werner Forman/Universal Images Group/Getty Images

55

HORUS

Horus, also spelled Hor, Har, Her, or Heru, was a god in the form of a falcon whose right eye was the sun or morning star, representing power and quintessence, and whose left eye was the moon or evening star, representing healing. Falcon cults, which were in evidence from late pre-dynastic times, were widespread in Egypt.

Horus appeared as a local god in many places and under different names and epithets—for instance, as Harmakhis (Har-em-akhet, "Horus in the Horizon"), Harpocrates (Har-pe-khrad, "Horus the Child"), Harsiesis (Har-si-Ese, "Horus, Son of Isis"), Harakhte ("Horus of the Horizon, "closely associated with the sun god Re), and, at Kawm Umbu (Kom Ombo), as Haroeris (Harwer, "Horus the Elder").

At Nekhen (Greek: Hierakonpolis), however, the conception arose that the reigning king was a manifestation of Horus, and, after Lower Egypt and Upper Egypt had been united by the kings from Nekhen, this notion became a generally accepted dogma. The most important of an Egyptian king's names (the number of which grew from three in Early Dynastic times to five later) was his Horus name—i.e., the name that identified him with Horus. This name appeared on monuments and tombs in a rectangular frame called a serekh.

In addition to being characterized by a Horus name, the king was typically depicted with a hovering form of Horus above his head. Sometimes Horus is shown as a winged sun disc, representing the Horus of Behdet, a

Statue of Horus at his temple in Idfū, Egypt. © Comstock/Jupiterimages

BA AND KA

In ancient Egyptian religion, the ba, with the ka and the akh, was a principal aspect of the soul; the ba appears in bird form, thus expressing the mobility of the soul after death. Originally written with the sign of the jabiru bird and thought to be an attribute of only the god-king, the ba was later represented by a man-headed hawk, often depicted hovering over the mummies of kings and commoners alike.

The ka was a principal aspect of the soul of a human being or of a god. The exact significance of the ka remains a matter of controversy, chiefly for lack of an Egyptian definition; the usual translation, "double," is incorrect. Written by a hieroglyph of uplifted arms, it seemed originally to have designated the protecting divine spirit of a person. The ka survived the death of the body and could reside in a picture or statue of a person.

town in the Nile River delta where the falcon-god enjoyed a cult.

From the 1st dynasty (c. 2925–2775 BCE) onward, Horus and the god Seth were presented as perpetual antagonists who were reconciled in the harmony of Upper and Lower Egypt. In the myth of Osiris, who became prominent about 2350 BCE, Horus was the son of Osiris and Isis and was the nephew of Seth, Osiris's brother. When Seth murdered Osiris and contested Horus's heritage (the royal throne of Egypt), Horus became Seth's enemy. Horus eventually defeated Seth, thus avenging his father and assuming the rule. In the fight, Horus's left eye (i.e., the moon) was damaged—this being a mythical explanation of the moon's phases—and was healed by the god Thoth. The figure of the restored eye (the wedjat eye) became a powerful amulet. Horus is also associated (sometimes as son, sometimes as partner) with the ancient cow-goddess Hathor, who is often depicted with cow's horns, sometimes with cow's ears.

In the Ptolemaic period the vanquishing of Seth became a symbol of Egypt triumphing over its occupiers. At Idfu, where rebellions frequently interrupted work on the temple, a ritual drama depicting Horus as pharaoh spearing Seth in the guise of a hippopotamus was periodically enacted.

Horus was later identified by the Greeks with Apollo, and the town of Idfu was called Apollinopolis ("Apollo's Town") during the Greco-Roman period.

ISIS

Also known as Aset or Eset, Isis was one of the most important goddesses of ancient Egypt. Her name is the Greek form of an ancient Egyptian word for "throne."

Isis was initially an obscure goddess who lacked her own dedicated temples, but she grew in importance as the dynastic age progressed, until she became one of the most important deities of ancient Egypt. Her cult subsequently spread throughout the Roman Empire, and Isis was worshipped from England to Afghanistan. She is still revered by pagans today. As mourner, she was a principal deity in rites connected with the dead; as magical healer, she cured the sick and brought the deceased to life; and as mother, she was a role model for all women.

Isis had strong links with Egyptian kingship, and she was most often represented as a beautiful woman wearing a sheath dress and either the hieroglyphic sign of the throne or a solar disc and cow's horns on her head. Occasionally she was represented as a scorpion, a bird, a sow, or a cow. There are no references to Isis before the 5th dynasty (2465–2325 BCE), but she is mentioned many times in the Pyramid Texts (c. 2350), in which she offers assistance to the

Limestone relief of King Nectanebo II (right) *welcomed by the goddess Isis, located in Saqqara, Egypt.* DEA/G. Dagli Orti/De Agostini/ Getty Images

dead king. Later, as ideas of the afterlife became more democratic, Isis was able to extend her help to all dead Egyptians.

The priests of Heliopolis, followers of the sun god Re, developed the myth of Isis. This told that Isis was the daughter of Earth god Geb and the sky goddess Nut and the sister of the deities Osiris, Seth, and Nephthys. Married to Osiris, king of Egypt, Isis was a good queen who supported her husband and taught the women of Egypt how to weave, bake, and brew beer. But Seth was jealous, and he hatched a plot to kill his brother. Seth trapped Osiris in a decorated wooden chest, which he coated in lead and threw into the Nile. The chest had become Osiris's coffin. With his brother vanished, Seth became king of Egypt. But Isis could not forget her husband, and she searched everywhere for him until she eventually discovered Osiris, still trapped in his chest, in Byblos. She brought his body back to Egypt, where Seth discovered the chest and,

BUCHIS

In ancient Egyptian religion, Buchis, a white bull with black markings, was worshipped as a favourite incarnation of the war god Mont. He was represented with the solar disc and two tall plumes between his horns. According to Macrobius, his hair grew in the opposite direction from that of ordinary animals and changed colour every hour. At Hermonthis (present-day Armant) in Upper Egypt, a special centre of Mont's worship, a particular bull was chosen to receive a cult as Buchis. Upon its death, it was mummified and buried in a sarcophagus with divine honours. The mothers of these Buchis bulls received a similar cult and burial.

furious, hacked his brother into pieces, which he scattered far and wide. Transforming into a bird, and helped by her sister, Nephthys, Isis was able to discover and reunite the parts of her dead husband's body—only his penis was missing. Using her magical powers, she was able to make Osiris whole; bandaged, neither living nor dead, Osiris had become a mummy. Nine months later Isis bore him a son, Horus. Osiris was then forced to retreat to the underworld, where he became king of the dead.

Isis hid with Horus in the marshes of the Nile delta until her son was fully grown and could avenge his father and claim his throne. She defended the child against attacks from snakes and scorpions. But because Isis was also Seth's sister, she wavered during the eventual battle between Horus and Seth. In one episode Isis took pity on Seth and was in consequence beheaded by Horus (the beheading was reversed by magic). Eventually she and Horus were reconciled, and Horus was able to take the throne of Egypt.

Isis was the perfect traditional Egyptian wife and mother—content to stay in the background while things went well, but able to use her wits to guard her husband and son should the need arise. The shelter she afforded her child gave her the character of a goddess of protection. But her chief aspect was that of a great magician, whose power transcended that of all other deities. Several narratives tell of her magical prowess, far stronger than the powers of Osiris and Re. She was frequently invoked on behalf of the sick, and, with the goddesses Nephthys, Neith, and Selket, she protected the dead. Isis became associated with various other goddesses, including Bastet, Nut, and Hathor, and thus her nature and her powers became increasingly diverse.

Isis became known, like other fierce goddesses in the Egyptian pantheon, as the "Eye of Re" and was equated with the Dog Star, Sothis (Sirius).

The first major temple dedicated to Isis was built by the Late period king Nectanebo II (360–343 BCE) at Behbeit el-Hagar, in the central Nile delta. Other important temples, including the island temple of Philae, were built during Greco-Roman times when Isis was dominant among Egyptian goddesses. Several temples were dedicated to her in Alexandria, where she became the patroness of seafarers. From Alexandria her cult spread to Greece and Rome. Images of Isis nursing the baby Horus may have influenced the early Christian artists who depicted the Virgin Mary with the baby Jesus.

KHNUM

Khnum, also spelled Khnemu, was the god of fertility, associated with water and with procreation. Khnum

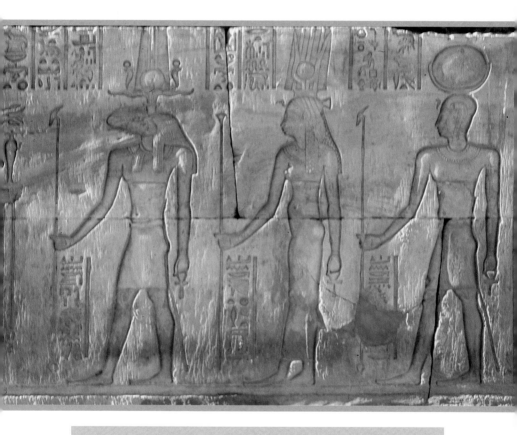

Relief depicting the gods (left to right) *Khnum, Hathor, and Horus.* Werner Forman/Universal Images Group/Getty Images

was worshipped from the 1st dynasty (*c*. 2925–2775 BCE) into the early centuries CE. He was represented as a ram with horizontal twisting horns or as a man with a ram's head. Khnum was believed to have created humankind from clay like a potter; this scene, with him using a potter's wheel, was depicted in later times. The god's first main cult centre was Herwer, near Al-Ashmunayn in Middle Egypt. From the New Kingdom (1539–1075 BCE) on, however, he was the god of the island of Elephantine, near present-day Aswan, and was known as the lord of the surrounding First Cataract of the Nile River. At Elephantine he formed a triad of deities with the goddesses Satis and Anukis. Khnum also had an important cult at Esna, south of Thebes.

KHONS

Khons, also spelled Khonsu or Chons, was the moon god who was generally depicted as a youth. A deity with astronomical associations named Khenzu is known from the Pyramid Texts (*c.* 2350 BCE) and is possibly the same as Khons. In Egyptian mythology, Khons was regarded as the son of the god Amon and the goddess Mut. In the period of the late New Kingdom (*c.* 1100 BCE), a major temple was built for Khons in the Karnak complex at Thebes. Khons was generally depicted as a young man with a side lock of hair; on his head he wore a uraeus (rearing cobra) and a lunar disc. Khons also was associated with baboons and was sometimes assimilated to Thoth, another moon god associated with baboons.

THE ROLE OF MAAT IN EGYPTIAN LIFE

Maat, also spelled Mayet, was the personification of truth, justice, and the cosmic order. The daughter of the sun god Re, she was associated with Thoth, god of wisdom.

The ceremony of judgment of the dead (called the "Judgment of Osiris," named for Osiris, the god of the dead) was believed to focus upon the weighing of the heart of the deceased in a scale balanced by Maat (or her hieroglyph, the ostrich feather), as a test of conformity to proper values.

In its abstract sense, maat was the divine order established at creation and reaffirmed at the accession of each new king of Egypt. In setting maat "order" in place of isfet "disorder," the king played the role of the sun god, the god with the closest links to Maat. Maat stood at the head of the sun god's bark as it traveled through the sky and the underworld. Although aspects of kingship and of maat were at times subjected to criticism and reformulation, the principles underlying these two institutions were fundamental to ancient Egyptian life and thought and endured to the end of ancient Egyptian history.

The concept of maat ("order") was fundamental in Egyptian thought. Maat was crucial in human life and embraced notions of reciprocity, justice, truth, and moderation. Maat was personified as a goddess and the creator's daughter and received a cult of her own. In the cult of other deities, the king's offering of

The goddess Maat from the Tomb of Nefertari. Kenneth Garrett/
National Geographic Image Collection/Getty Images

maat to a deity encapsulated the relationship between humanity, the king, and the gods; as the representative of humanity, he returned to the gods the order that came from them and of which they were themselves part. Maat extended into the world of the dead: in the weighing of the heart after death, shown on papyri deposited in burials, the person's heart occupies one side of the scales and a representation of maat the other. The meaning of this image is deepened in the accompanying text, which asserts that the deceased behaved correctly on earth and did not overstep the boundaries of order, declaring that he or she did not "know that which is not"—that is, things that were outside the created and ordered world.

This role of maat in human life created a continuity between religion, political action, and elite morality. Over the centuries, private religion and morality drew apart from state concerns, paralleling a gradual separation of king and temple. It cannot be known whether religion and morality were as closely integrated for the people as they were for the elite, or even how fully the elite subscribed to these beliefs. Nonetheless, the integration of cosmos, king, and maat remained fundamental.

MIN

Min was a god of fertility and harvest, and the embodiment of the masculine principle; he was also worshipped as the Lord of the Eastern Desert. His cult originated in pre-dynastic times (4th millennium BCE). Min was represented with phallus erect, a flail in his raised right hand. His cult was strongest in Coptos and Akhmim (Panopolis), where in his honour great festivals were held celebrating his "coming forth," with public processions and presentation of offerings. The lettuce was his sacred plant.

MNEVIS

M nevis was a sacred bull deity worshipped at Heliopolis. As one of several sacred bulls in Egypt, he was most closely associated with the sun god Re-Atum. Although not attested with certainty until the Middle Kingdom (1938–c. 1630 BCE), the Mnevis bull may be that which is referenced by the phrase "bull of Heliopolis," which occurs in the Pyramid Texts. The Mnevis bull was either black or piebald in colour, and in sculptures and paintings he was represented with a solar disc between his horns.

MONT

Also spelled Montu, Monthu, or Mentu, Mont was a god of the 4th Upper Egyptian nome (province), whose original capital of Hermonthis (present-day Armant) was replaced by Thebes during the 11th dynasty (2081–1939 BCE). Mont was a god of war. In addition to falcons, a bull was his sacred animal; from the 30th dynasty (380–343 BCE), this bull, the Buchis bull, received an elaborate cult. Mont was represented as a man with a falcon's head, wearing a crown of two plumes with a double uraeus (rearing cobra) on his forehead. He had important temple complexes at Karnak in Thebes and at Hermonthis, Al-Tud, and Al-Madamud in the Theban area, all of which expanded greatly in the period of Roman rule.

EGYPTIAN MYTHOLOGY'S INFLUENCE ON OTHER RELIGIONS

Egyptian culture, of which religion was an integral part, was influential in Nubia as early as pre-dynastic times and in Syria in the 3rd millennium BCE. During the New Kingdom, Egypt was very receptive to cults from the Middle East, while Egyptian medical and magical expertise was highly regarded among the Hittites, Assyrians, and Babylonians. The chief periods of Egyptian influence were, however, the 1st millennium BCE and the Roman period. Egypt was an important centre of the Jewish diaspora starting in the 6th century BCE, and Egyptian literature influenced the Hebrew Bible. With Greek rule there was significant cultural interchange between Egyptians and Greeks. Notable among Egyptian cults that spread abroad were those of Isis, which reached much of the Roman world as a mystery religion, and of Serapis, a god whose name probably derives from Osiris-Apis, who was worshipped widely in a non-Egyptian iconography and cultural milieu. With Isis went Osiris and Horus the child, but Isis was the dominant figure. Many Egyptian monuments were imported to Rome to provide a setting for the principal Isis temple in the 1st century CE.

The cult of Isis was probably influential on another level. The myth of Osiris shows some analogies with the Gospel story and, in the figure of Isis, with the role of the Virgin Mary. The iconography of the Virgin and Child has evident affinities with that of Isis and the infant Horus. Thus, one aspect of Egyptian religion may have contributed to the background of early Christianity, probably through the cultural centre of Alexandria. Egypt also was an influential setting for other religious and philosophical developments of late antiquity such as Gnosticism, Manichaeism, Hermetism, and Neoplatonism, some of which show traces of traditional Egyptian beliefs. Some of these religions became important in the intellectual culture of the Renaissance. Finally, Christian monasticism seems to have originated in Egypt and could look back to a range of native practices, among which were seclusion in temple precincts and the celibacy of certain priestesses. Within Egypt, there are many survivals from earlier times in popular Christianity and Islam.

MUT

Mut was a sky goddess and great divine mother. Mut is thought to have originated in the Nile River delta or in Middle Egypt. She came to prominence during the 18th dynasty (1539–1292 BCE) as the companion of the god Amonat Thebes, forming the Theban triad with him and with the youthful god Khons, who was said to be Mut's son. The name "Mut" means "mother," and her role was that of an older woman among the gods. She was associated with the uraeus (rearing cobra), lionesses, and royal crowns.

At Thebes the principal festival of Mut was her "navigation" on the distinctive horseshoe-shaped lake, or Isheru, that surrounded her temple complex at Karnak. Mut was usually represented as a woman wearing the double crown (of Upper and Lower Egypt) typically worn by the king and by the god Atum. She was also occasionally depicted with the head of a lioness, particularly when identified with other goddesses, principally Bastet and Sekhmet.

Limestone bust of the goddess Mut.
Album/Prisma/SuperStock

NEFERTEM

Also spelled Nefertum, or Nefertemu, Nefertem was a youthful god associated with the lotus flower. Nefertem was an ancient god, mentioned in the Pyramid Texts (*c.* 2350 BCE), but he became more prominent during the New Kingdom (1539–*c.* 1075 BCE) and later. As a blue lotus he was believed to have emerged from the primeval waters. He also had a warlike aspect and could be depicted as a lion. He was most commonly represented holding a scimitar with a falcon's head and wearing a headdress of a lotus with a menat (ritual necklace counterpoise) on each side and a pair of plumes above. As the son of Ptah and Sekhmet, he formed part of the Memphite Triad.

NEITH

Neith, also spelled Neit, was the patroness of the city of Sais in the Nile River delta. Neith was worshipped as early as pre-dynastic times (*c.* 3000 BCE), and several queens of the 1st dynasty (*c.* 2925–2775 BCE) were named after her. She also became an important goddess in the capital city of Memphis. Her principal emblem was a pair of crossed arrows shown against the background of a leather shield. A further emblem was a bow case, which the goddess was sometimes depicted wearing on her head in place of a crown. But Neith was usually depicted as a woman wearing the red crown associated with Lower Egypt, holding crossed arrows and a bow. In mythology she was the mother of the crocodile god, Sebek, and later of Re. The worship of Neith was particularly prominent in the 26th dynasty (664–525 BCE), when Egypt's capital was located at Sais.

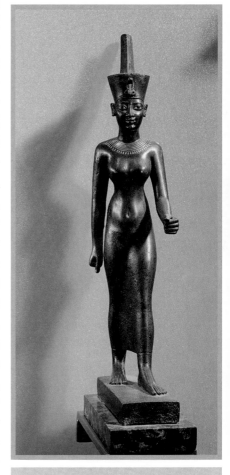

Figurine of Neith. DEA Picture Library/Getty Images

NEKHBET

Nekhbet was the vulture goddess who was the protector of Upper Egypt and especially its rulers.

Nekhbet was frequently portrayed as spreading her wings over the pharaoh while grasping in her claw the cartouche symbol or other emblems. She also appeared as a woman, often with a vulture's head, wearing a white crown, and was sometimes depicted suckling the pharaoh. The centre of Nekhbet's cult was El-Kab (Greek: Eileithyiaspolis), but her principal epithet made her the goddess of Hierakonpolis (or Nekhen), the ancient town opposite El-Kab, on the west bank of the Nile River.

Nekhbet hovering over Menkauhor, Egypt, 25th–24th century BCE.
Alinari/Art Resource, New York

ANIMAL MANIFESTATIONS OF GODS

Deities had principal manifestations, and most were associated with one or more species of animal. For gods the most important forms were the falcon and bull, and for goddesses the cow, cobra, vulture, and lioness. Rams were widespread, while some manifestations were as modest as the millipede of the god Sepa. Some gods were very strongly linked to particular animals, as Sebek was with the crocodile and Khepri with the scarab beetle. Thoth had two animals, the ibis and the baboon. Some animal cults were only partly integrated with specific gods, notably the Ram of Mendes in the delta and the Apis and Mnevis bulls at Memphis and Heliopolis, respectively. Animals could express aspects of a deity's nature: some goddesses were lionesses in their fiercer aspect but were cats when mild.

Relief depicting a dead man making an offering to the bull Apis while Isis spreads her wings in protection. Werner Forman/Universal Images Group/Getty Images

These variable forms relate to aspects of the person that were common to gods and people. The most significant of these were the ka, which was the vital essence of a person that was transmitted from one generation to the next, the ba, which granted freedom of movement and the ability to take on different forms, principally in the next world, and the akh, the transfigured spirit of a person in the next world.

NUN

Nun, also spelled Nu, was the oldest of the ancient Egyptian gods and father of Re, the sun god. Nun's name means "primeval waters," and he represented the waters of chaos out of which Re-Atum began creation. Nun's qualities were boundlessness, darkness, and the turbulence of stormy waters; these qualities were personified separately by pairs of deities. Nun, his female counterpart, Naunet, and three further pairs together formed the Ogdoad (group of eight gods) of Hermopolis. Various Egyptian creation myths retain the image of the emergence of a primeval hillock formed of mud churned from the chaotic waters of Nun. Since it was believed that the primeval ocean continued to surround the ordered cosmos, the creation myth was reenacted each day as the sun god rose from the waters of chaos. Nun was also thought to continue to exist as the source of the annual flooding of the Nile River.

RECORDING OF MYTHS

Myths are poorly known. Religious discourse was recorded in hymns, rituals, temple scenes, and specialized texts but rarely in narrative, which only slowly became a common written genre and never had the highest literary prestige. In addition, much religious activity focused on constant reiteration or repetition rather than on development. A central example of this tendency is the presentation of the cycle of the sun god through the sky and the underworld, which was an analogy for the creation, maturity, decay, and regeneration of an individual life and of the cosmos. This is strikingly presented in the underworld books. These pictorial and textual compositions, which probably imparted secret knowledge, were inscribed in the tombs of New Kingdom kings. They describe the solar cycle in great detail, including hundreds of names of demons and of deities and other beings who accompanied the sun god in his barque on his journey through night and day. The texts are in the present tense and form a description and a series of tableaux rather than a narrative.

The fact that mythical narratives are rare does not imply that myths or narratives did not exist. There is reason to think that some myths underlay features of enneads and therefore had originated by the Early Dynastic period (c. 3000 BCE). Mythical narratives preserved from the New Kingdom and later include episodes of the rule of the sun god on Earth, tales of the childhood of Horus in the delta marshes, and stories with themes similar to the Osiris myth but with differently named protagonists. The rule of the sun god was followed by his withdrawal into the sky, leaving people on Earth. The withdrawal was motivated by his age and by the lack of tranquility in the world. One narrative recounts how Isis obtained a magical substance from Re's senile dribbling and fashioned from it a snake that bit him; to make her still the agony of the snakebite, he finally revealed to her the secret of his "true" name. A myth with varied realizations recounts how Re grew weary of humanity's recalcitrance and dispatched his daughter or "Eye" to destroy them. Regretting his action later, he arranged to have the bloodthirsty goddess tricked into drunkenness by spreading beer tinted the colour of blood over the land. This myth provides an explanation for the world's imperfection and the inaccessibility of the gods. In Greco-Roman times it was widespread in Lower Nubia, where it seems to have been related to the winter retreat of the sun to the Southern Hemisphere and its return in the spring.

NUT

Nut was a goddess of the sky, vault of the heavens, often depicted as a woman arched over Earth god Geb. Most cultures of regions where there is rain personify the sky as masculine, the rain being the seed that fructifies Mother Earth. In Egypt, however, rain plays no role in fertility; all the useful water is on Earth (from the Nile River). Egyptian religion is unique in the genders of its deities of Earth and sky. As the goddess of the sky, Nut

A detail of the painted sarcophagus of Butehamun illustrating Shu holding Nut, separating her from Geb. Werner Forman/Universal Images Group/Getty Images

OPET

Opet was the ancient Egyptian festival of the second month of the lunar calendar. In the celebration of Opet, the god Amon, Mut, his consort, and Khons, their son, made a ritual journey from their shrines at Karnak to the Temple of Luxor (called *Ipet resyt* in pharaonic Egyptian, hence the name of the festival). Scenes of the festival in the Colonnade of the Temple of Luxor carved during Tutankhamen's reign (1333–23 BCE) show priests carrying statues of Amon, Mut, and Khons in barks through the streets of ancient Thebes, thence onto river barges and on to Luxor. Following this appearance to the populace, the statues remained in the Temple of Luxor for about 24 days, during which the city remained in festival. The images were returned by the same route to their shrines in Karnak in a second public appearance that closed the festival. A direct survival of the ancient cult is seen in the present-day feast of the Muslim holy man Sheikh Yusuf al-Haggag, whose boat is carried about Luxor amid popular celebration. His mosque stands in the northeastern corner of the first court of the Temple of Luxor, over the foundations of a Byzantine church.

Through an association with Mut, the name Opet (or Apet) was also applied to a local city goddess of Thebes, who was depicted in a manner similar to that of Taurt, the hippopotamus goddess of fertility and childbirth.

swallowed the sun in the evening and gave birth to it again in the morning.

Nut was also represented as a cow, for this was the form she took in order to carry the sun god Re on her back to the sky. On five special days preceding the New Year, Nut gave birth successively to the deities Osiris, Horus, Seth, Isis, and Nephthys. These gods, with the exception of Horus, were commonly referred to as the "children of Nut."

OSIRIS

O siris, also called Usir, was one of the most important gods of ancient Egypt. The origin of Osiris is obscure; he was a local god of Busiris, in Lower Egypt, and may have been a personification of chthonic (underworld) fertility. By about 2400 BCE, however, Osiris clearly played a double role: he was both a god of fertility and the embodiment of the dead and resurrected king. This dual role was in turn combined with the Egyptian concept of divine kingship: the king at death became Osiris, god of the underworld; and the dead king's son, the living king, was identified with Horus, a god of the sky. Osiris and Horus were thus father and son. The goddess Isis was the mother of the king and was thus the mother of Horus and consort of Osiris. The god Seth was considered the murderer of Osiris and adversary of Horus.

According to the form of the myth reported by the Greek author Plutarch, Osiris was slain or drowned by Seth, who tore the corpse into 14 pieces and flung them over Egypt. Eventually, Isis and her sister Nephthys found and buried all the pieces, except the phallus, thereby giving new life to Osiris, who thenceforth remained in the underworld as ruler and judge. His son Horus successfully fought against Seth, avenging Osiris and becoming the new king of Egypt.

Osiris was not only ruler of the dead but also the power that granted all life from the underworld, from sprouting vegetation to the annual flood of the Nile River. From about 2000 BCE onward it was believed that every man, not just the deceased kings, became associated with

Relief of Osiris in the Ptolemaic Temple of Hathor and Maat, Deir el-Medina, Egypt. Universal Images Group/Getty Images

Osiris at death. This identification with Osiris, however, did not imply resurrection, for even Osiris did not rise from the dead. Instead, it signified the renewal of life both in the next world and through one's descendants on Earth. In this universalized form Osiris's cult spread throughout Egypt, often joining with the cults of local fertility and underworld deities.

The idea that rebirth in the next life could be gained by following Osiris was maintained through certain cult forms. In the Middle Kingdom (1938–c. 1630 BCE) the god's festivals consisted of processions and nocturnal rites and were celebrated at the temple of Abydos, where Osiris had assimilated the very ancient god of the dead, Khenty-Imentiu. This name, meaning "Foremost of the Westerners," was adopted by Osiris as an epithet. Because the festivals took place in the open, public participation was permitted, and by the early 2nd millennium BCE it had become fashionable to be buried along the processional road at Abydos or to erect a cenotaph there as a representative of the dead.

Osiris festivals symbolically reenacting the god's fate were celebrated annually in various towns throughout Egypt. A central feature of the festivals during the late period was the construction of the "Osiris garden," a mold in the shape of Osiris, filled with soil. The mold was moistened with the water of the Nile and sown with grain. Later, the sprouting grain symbolized the vital strength of Osiris.

At Memphis the holy bull, Apis, was linked with Osiris, becoming Osiris-Apis, which eventually became the name of the Hellenistic god Serapis. Greco-Roman authors connected Osiris with the god Dionysus. Osiris was also identified with Soker, an ancient Memphite god of the dead.

GREEKS, ROMANS, AND ANCIENT EGYPT

The only extensive contemporaneous descriptions of ancient Egyptian culture from the outside were made by Classical Greek and Roman writers. Their works include many important observations about Egyptian religion, which particularly interested the writers and which until late antiquity was not fundamentally different in type from their own religions. Herodotus (5th century BCE) remarked that the Egyptians were the most religious of people, and the comment is apt because popular religious practices proliferated in the 1st millennium BCE. Other significant Classical sources include Plutarch's essay on Isis and Osiris (1st century CE), which gives the only known connected narrative of their myth, and the writings of Apuleius (2nd century CE) and others about the Isis cult as it spread in the Greco-Roman world.

The oldest known depiction of Osiris dates to about 2300 BCE, but representations of him are rare before the New Kingdom (1539–1075 BCE), when he was shown in an archaizing form as a mummy with his arms crossed on his breast, one hand holding a crook, the other a flail. On his head was the atef-crown, composed of the white crown of Upper Egypt and two ostrich feathers.

PTAH

Ptah, also spelled Phthah, was a creator-god and maker of things, a patron of craftsmen, especially sculptors; his high priest was called "chief controller of craftsmen." The Greeks identified Ptah with Hephaestus (Vulcan), the divine blacksmith. Ptah was originally the local deity of Memphis, capital of Egypt from the 1st dynasty onward; the political importance of Memphis caused Ptah's cult to expand over the whole of Egypt. With his companion Sekhmet and the youthful god Nefertem, he was one of the Memphite Triad of deities. He was represented as a man in mummy form, wearing a skullcap and a short, straight false beard. As a mortuary god, Ptah was often fused with Seker (or Soker) and Osiris to form Ptah-Seker-Osiris. The sacred bull Apis had his stall in the great temple of Ptahat Memphis and was called a manifestation of the god who gave oracles.

Gold statue of Ptah, found in the tomb of Tutankhamun. Werner Forman/Universal Images Group/Getty Images

RE

Also spelled Ra, or Pra, Re was the god of the sun and creator god. He was believed to travel across the sky in his solar bark and, during the night, to make his passage in another bark through the underworld, where, in order to be born again for the new day, he had to vanquish the evil serpent Apopis (Apepi). As one of the creator gods, he rose from the ocean of chaos on the primeval hill, creating himself and then in turn engendering eight other gods.

The sun god Re with falcon head, journeying through the underworld.
Werner Forman/Universal Images Group/Getty Images

SEBEK

Sebek, also spelled Sobek, was the crocodile god whose chief sanctuary in Fayyum province included a live sacred crocodile, Petsuchos (Greek: "He Who Belongs to Suchos"), in whom the god was believed to be incarnate.

Sebek may have been an early fertility god or associated with death and burial before becoming a major deity and patron of kings in the Middle Kingdom (c. 1938–c. 1630 BCE). He was merged with Re, the sun god, to constitute a crocodile form of that god known as Sebek-Re. The worship of Sebek continued into Ptolemaic and Roman times in the Fayyum, at Kawm Umbu (Kom Ombo) in Upper Egypt, and elsewhere. Cemeteries of mummified crocodiles have been found in the Fayyum and at Kawm Umbu.

SEKHMET

Also spelled Sakhmet, Sekhmet was a goddess of war and the destroyer of the enemies of the sun god Re. Sekhmet was associated both with disease and with healing and medicine. Like other fierce goddesses in the Egyptian pantheon, she was called the "Eye of Re." She was the companion of the god Ptah and was worshipped principally at Memphis. She was usually depicted as a lioness or as a woman with the head of a lioness, on which was placed the solar disc and the uraeus serpent. Sekhmet was sometimes identified with other Egyptian goddesses, such as Hathor, Bastet, and Mut.

Seated figure of Sekhmet from the tomb of Tutankhamun. Werner Forman/Universal Images Group/Getty Images

SELKET

Selket, also spelled Selqet, or Serqet, was a goddess of the dead. Her symbolic animal was the scorpion. She was one of the underworld deities charged with protecting the canopic jar in which the intestines of the deceased were stored after embalming.

SHU

Shu was god of the air and supporter of the sky, created by Atum by his own power, without the aid of a woman. Shu and his sister and companion, Tefnut (goddess of moisture), were the first couple of the group of nine gods called the Ennead of Heliopolis. Of their union were born Geb, the Earth god, and Nut, the goddess of the sky. Shu was portrayed in human form with the hieroglyph of his name, an ostrich feather, on his head. He was often represented separating Geb and Nut, supporting with uplifted arms the body of Nut arched above him. In some Middle Kingdom texts Shu was given the status of a primeval creator god. Later he was frequently termed the "Son of Re" (the sun god), and he was also identified with Onuris, a warrior god, thus acquiring martial associations.

THOTH

Thoth was a god of the moon, of reckoning, of learning, and of writing. He was held to be the inventor of writing, the creator of languages, the scribe, interpreter, and adviser of the gods, and the representative of the sun god, Re. His responsibility for writing was shared with the

Statue of Thoth, represented as a striding man with bronze ibis head. Werner Forman/Universal Images Group/Getty Images

goddess Seshat. The cult of Thoth was centred in the town of Khmunu (Hermopolis; modern Al-Ashmunayn) in Upper Egypt.

In the myth of Osiris, Thoth protected Isis during her pregnancy and healed the eye of her son, Horus, which had been wounded by Osiris's adversary Seth. He weighed the hearts of the deceased at their judgment and reported the result to the presiding god, Osiris, and his fellow judges. Thoth's sacred animals were the ibis and the baboon; millions of mummified bodies of those animals have been found in cemeteries near Hermopolis and Memphis. Thoth was usually represented in human form with an ibis's head. The Greeks identified Thoth with their god Hermes and termed him "Thoth, the thrice great" (Hermes Trismegistos). Important philosophical works were attributed to Hermes Trismegistos.

WADJET

Wadjet, also spelled Wadjit, was the cobra goddess of ancient Egypt. Depicted as a cobra twined around a papyrus stem, she was the tutelary goddess of Lower Egypt. Wadjet and Nekhbet, the vulture-goddess of Upper Egypt, were the protective goddesses of the king and were sometimes represented together on the king's diadem, symbolizing his reign over all of Egypt. The form of the rearing cobra on a crown is termed the uraeus. In mythology, Wadjet was nurse to the infant god Horus and helped Isis, his mother, protect him from his treacherous uncle, Seth, when she took refuge in the delta swamps. The similarity of this myth to the Greek story of Leto and Apollo on Delos probably resulted in the later identification of Wadjet with Leto.

GLOSSARY

abstruse Difficult to comprehend.

allegorical Having hidden spiritual meaning that transcends the literal sense of a sacred text.

amulet A charm (as an ornament) often inscribed with a magic incantation or symbol to aid the wearer or protect against evil (as disease or witchcraft).

antagonist One that contends with or opposes another.

benevolence Disposition to do good.

decorum Propriety and good taste in conduct or appearance.

deity One exalted or revered as supremely good or powerful.

demotic Of, relating to, or written in a simplified form of the ancient Egyptian hieratic writing.

diadem Something that adorns like a crown.

manifestation An occurrence that is readily perceived by the senses and especially by the sense of sight.

microcosm A community or other unity that is an epitome of a larger unity.

necropolis A large elaborate cemetery of an ancient city.

officiant One (as a priest) who presides over a religious rite.

oracle A person through whom a deity is believed to speak.

papyrus The pith of the papyrus plant, especially when made into strips and pressed into a material to write on.

phonetic Of or relating to spoken language or speech sounds.

pillage The act of looting or plundering, especially in war.

plurality The state of being numerous.

polytheism Belief in or worship of more than one god.

protagonist A leading actor, character, or participant in a literary work or real event.

reciprocity Mutual dependence, action, or influence.

sacerdotal Of or relating to priests or a priesthood.

sarcophagus A stone coffin.

schema A diagrammatic presentation.

scimitar A saber having a curved blade with the edge on the convex side.

stele A usually carved or inscribed stone slab or pillar used for commemorative purposes.

syncretism The combination of different forms of belief or practice.

tableaux A graphic description or representation.

FOR FURTHER READING

Adamson, Heather. *Ancient Egypt: An Interactive History Adventure*. Mankato, MN: Capstone, 2010.

Boyer, Crispin. *National Geographic Kids Everything Ancient Egypt*. Washington, DC: National Geographic, 2011.

Cotterell, Arthur. *The Illustrated Guide to the Mythology of the World: Ancient Greek, Roman, Egyptian, Norse, Chinese, Indian and Japanese*. London, England: Lorenz, 2011.

Dalley, Stephanie. *Myths from Mesopotamia: Creation, the Flood, Gilgamesh, and Others*. Oxford, England: Oxford University Press, 2008.

Dell, Christopher. *Mythology: The Complete Guide to Our Imagined Worlds*. New York, NY: Thames & Hudson, 2012.

Forest, Christopher. *Ancient Egyptian Gods and Goddesses*. Mankato, MN: Capstone, 2012.

Green, Roger Lancelyn, and Heather Copley. *Tales of Ancient Egypt*. London, England: Puffin, 2011.

Hamilton, Edith. *Mythology: Timeless Tales of Gods and Heroes*. New York, NY: Grand Central, 2011.

Leeming, David Adams. *The Oxford Companion to World Mythology*. Oxford, England: Oxford University Press, 2005.

Napoli, Donna Jo. *Treasury of Egyptian Mythology: Classic Stories of Gods, Goddesses, Monsters & Mortals*. Washington, DC: National Geographic, 2013.

Thury, Eva M., and Margaret Klopfle Devinney. *Introduction to Mythology: Contemporary Approaches to Classical and World Myths*. Oxford, England: Oxford University Press, 2009.

Thury, Eva M., and Margaret Klopfle Devinney. *Introduction to Mythology: Contemporary Approaches to Classical and World Myths*. Oxford, England: Oxford University Press, 2013.

Wilkinson, Philip. *Myths & Legends*. New York, NY: DK Publishing, 2009.

Wilkinson, Toby A.H. *The Rise and Fall of Ancient Egypt*. New York, NY: Random House, 2013.

Williams, Marcia. *Ancient Egypt: Tales of Gods and Pharaohs*. Somerville, MA: Candlewick, 2011.

Witzel, Michael. *The Origins of the World's Mythologies*. Oxford, England: Oxford University Press, 2012.

INDEX

INDEX